Let's Explore
SPACE

Written by Simon Mugford

TOP THAT! Kids™

Published by Top That! Publishing plc
Tide Mill Way, Woodbridge, Suffolk, IP12 1AP, UK
www.topthatpublishing.com
Copyright © 2005 Top That! Publishing plc
Top That! Kids is a Trademark of Top That! Publishing plc

GETTING STARTED

This book is full of fascinating facts and figures about planets, stars, space rockets and more. The kit contains equipment to help you do the super space activities.

What's in the kit?
- paints • paintbrush
- glow-in-the-dark stars
- a star chart
- polystyrene balls
- thread
- double-sided tape
- mobile rods and connectors

Other things you'll need:
- old newspapers • scissors
- sticky tape • cardboard tubes
- card • PVA glue • string

You can buy all of these things in good craft or hobby shops.

Important things to remember...

Some of these activities are messy – cover your work surface with some old newspapers.

• Always ask before using anything from around the home.

• Ask an adult to help you with any cutting out.

• Adult supervision is recommended.

3

THE SOLAR SYSTEM

The Sun is a star. Nine planets travel around the Sun along paths called orbits. The Sun, planets, moons, asteroids, comets and other bits of rock and dust are all part of the solar system.

The Sun

The Sun is enormous – more than a million times bigger than the Earth.

Venus

Venus is a boiling hot planet about the same size as the Earth.

Mercury

This is the closest planet to the Sun.

Moon
The Moon orbits the Earth.

Earth
Our own world is the
third planet from the Sun.

Mars
Mars is a red, rocky planet
about half the size of Earth.

5

THE SOLAR SYSTEM

Jupiter
This is the biggest planet in the solar system. Jupiter is made mostly of gas and has a distinctive red 'eye'.

Saturn
The second largest planet, Saturn is surrounded by rings of ice and dust.

Uranus

This blue-green coloured planet is tilted over on its side. It has rings too, but they cannot be seen as clearly as Saturn's.

Neptune

Neptune is a beautiful blue colour, with streaks of white clouds around its centre.

Pluto

This planet is farthest from the Sun and is the smallest in the solar system.

SOLAR SYSTEM MOBILE

Follow the step-by-step instructions to make your very own model of the solar system.

You will need:
- paints • paintbrush
- polystyrene balls
- scissors
- rods and connectors
- a piece of cardboard
- thread cut into 30 cm lengths
- double-sided sticky tape

Step 1
Use the largest polystyrene ball for the Sun. Place one half-ball on a sheet of card and draw a circle round it. Draw a flame effect around the circle, then ask an adult to cut out the centre, and round the edges of the flames.

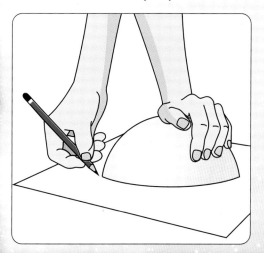

SOLAR SYSTEM MOBILE

Step 2

Stick the two halves of the ball together with the double-sided tape, trapping the end of one length of thread between them. Push the cardboard flames design over the ball and it will fit firmly around its centre.

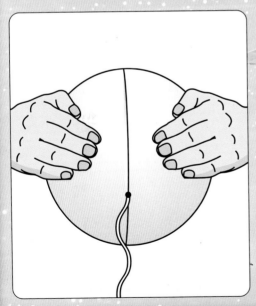

The Sun

Step 3

Cover the ball in the yellow paint from the kit. When this has dried, mix an orange by using the red and yellow paint and use this to paint on lots of swirly patterns. Leave to dry. You may like to add a thin coat of PVA glue to your Sun once the paint has dried, to enhance the colours and leave it looking glossy.

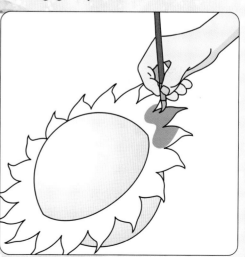

SOLAR SYSTEM MOBILE

Step 4

Make Jupiter and Saturn in the same way, using the second-largest balls. Then make Neptune and Uranus, using the third-largest balls. Look at the pictures on pages 6 and 7 to make sure you get the correct colours.

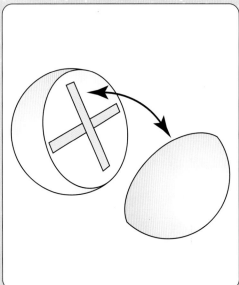

Jupiter

Saturn

Venus

Earth

Mars

Mercury

Pluto

Step 5

Use the fourth-largest balls to make Earth and Venus, and the fifth-largest ball to make Mars. Use the remaining two balls, (the smallest) to make Mercury and Pluto. Once they've been painted, leave them to dry thoroughly.

SOLAR SYSTEM MOBILE

Step 6

Cut a ring out of a piece of card, in the same way as the flames were created for the Sun, to make Saturn's rings, and paint it before sliding it into place.

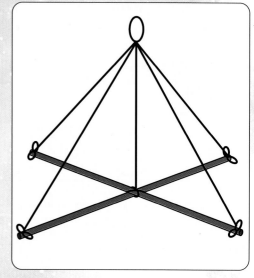

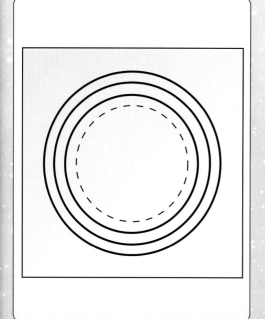

Step 7

Attach some thread to the rods, as shown. You will need to attach pieces of thread to the ends of each rod and one to the centre. When hanging the mobile, make sure all threads meet in the middle. To keep the rods level, make a loop for hanging and tie it tightly.

Step 8

Starting with the Sun in the middle, attach the planets along the length of the rods.

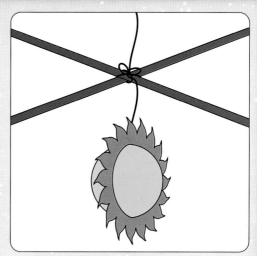

Step 9

Your model of the solar system is now ready to be hung up.

THE MOON

The Moon is often the biggest and the brightest thing that we can see in the night sky.

It is lit by light from the Sun.

The Moon appears to change shape as it orbits the Earth.

1.

1. New Moon
When the part of the Moon that is lit by the Sun is turned away from the Earth, we cannot see it. This is called a new Moon.

2.

2. Waxing Moon
As the Moon begins to be lit up, we can see a small part of it called a crescent. The Moon is said to be 'waxing'.

 3.

3. Full Moon
This is when we see the whole of the Moon lit up. A full Moon is seen once every 28 days.

4. Waning Moon
This Moon appears to shrink, or 'wane', as it continues its orbit and less of it is lit up.

 4.

MOON CHART

Make a chart to record the different phases of the Moon in a single month.

You will need:
- eight sheets of yellow paper
- a saucer or similar round object
- pen and pencil
- a glue stick or PVA glue
- a large sheet of black card
- glow-in-the-dark stars
- glitter

Step 1

Use the saucer to draw circles on each sheet of yellow paper. Ask an adult to cut out the shapes that represent the different phases of the Moon, as shown on page 18. Also ask them to cut out eight rectangles from the yellow paper and eight squares from one end of the black card.

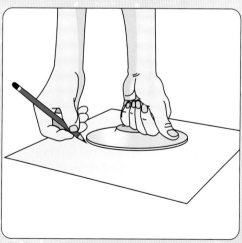

MOON CHART

Step 2

Use the glue to stick these shapes onto the piece of black card, as shown.

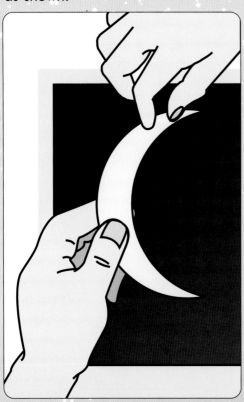

Step 3

Have a look at the Moon every night. Write the date in the rectangle below the shape which looks most like the Moon you can see.

Step 4

You should be able to record a complete cycle of the Moon over a month. Why not decorate your Moon chart with pictures of stars and planets? You could copy the template onto your card, covering the shapes with glue and sprinkling glitter onto them. Or you can use the glow-in-the-dark stars from the kit.

Saturday 2nd March	Tuesday 5th March
Saturday 9th March	Wednesday 13th March
Sunday 17th March	Thursday 21st March
Monday 25th March	Friday 29th March

SPACE ROCKETS

Rockets are the most powerful machines ever built. They are used to send spacecraft, satellites and people into space. Most rockets can be used only once.

A-class

A Russian A-class rocket carried Yuri Gagarin – the first human in space – in 1961.

Saturn V

The American Saturn V rockets carried the Apollo spacecraft and astronauts to the moon. They were the biggest rockets ever built.

Space Shuttle

The Space Shuttle is a special kind of rocket that can be used many times. The main part of the Shuttle is called the orbiter. When it returns to Earth, it lands on a runway like an aeroplane.

MODEL ROCKET

Follow the instructions to build your own model rocket.

You will need:

- thin card
- a long cardboard tube
- three short cardboard tubes
- strips of newspaper or
  kitchen towels • PVA glue
  - a bowl • paints
    - sticky tape
      - scissors

Step 1

First, you need to make the rocket's nose cone. On a piece of thin card, draw around a plate to make a circle about 10 cm across and cut it out.

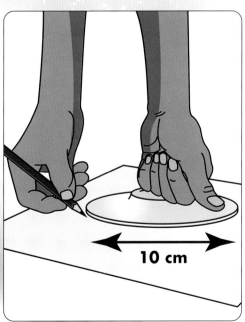

10 cm

MODEL ROCKET

Step 2

Cut a slit from the edge to the middle. Fold the circle into a cone shape, as shown in the picture below. Hold it in place with a piece of sticky tape.

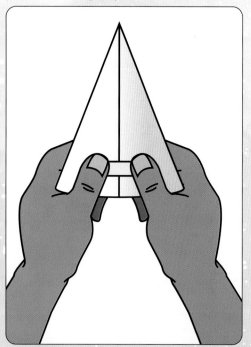

Step 3

With another piece of sticky tape, attach the paper cone to one end of the long cardboard tube, as shown in the picture below.

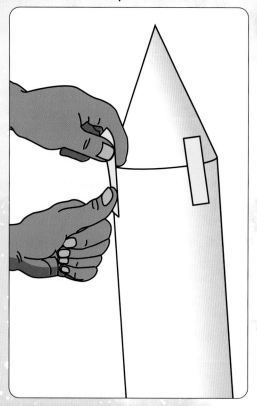

Step 4

Cut out three fins from the card. Cut five tabs to make it easier to attach them. Stick them to one end of the small tubes, as shown below, with three going one way and two going the other.

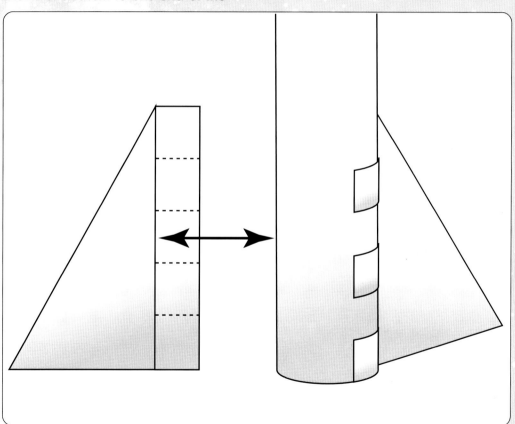

MODEL ROCKET

Step 5

Put some PVA glue in a bowl, add water slowly until the mixture looks like milk and mix together. Soak strips of newspaper or kitchen towel in this paste, squeeze out excess and stick them to the outside of the cardboard tubes, the cone and the fins. Apply 2–3 layers and leave to dry.

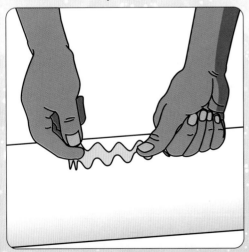

Step 6

When the tubes are dry, you can paint them. Look at the pictures of the rockets on pages 22–23 for some colour ideas.

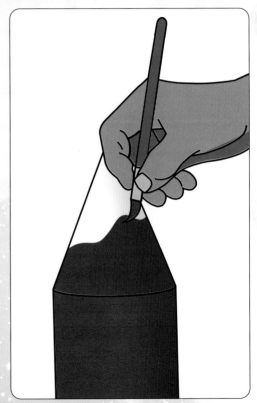

Step 7

When the paint is dry, use PVA glue to stick the three small tubes around the base of the long tube, as shown in the picture to the right.

Add some finishing touches such as sticking on pieces of silver foil or painting a name for your rocket on its side.

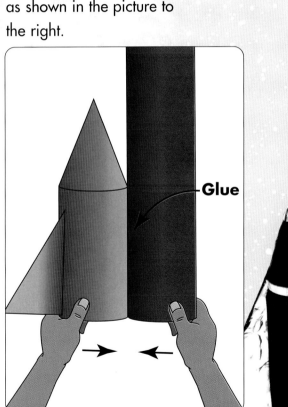

Glue

COMETS, METEORS AND MOONS

As well as the Sun, planets and stars, other things that fill the sky include comets, meteors and moons.

Our planet is not the only one with its own moon. Jupiter has many moons which were photographed by the Voyager spacecraft when it flew past the planet in 1979.

Comets make a spectacular sight in the night sky as they fly past the Earth. A comet has a core called a nucleus and is followed by a tail which can be made of gas or dust.

Meteorites are chunks of metal or rock floating around in space. Sometimes it is possible to see meteor showers, or shooting stars as they are known, from Earth.

Star Chart

What is a star chart?
For thousands of years sailors used star charts in the same way that drivers use road maps - to help them find their way. Although the stars are really huge distances apart, from Earth many of them appear to fall into recognisable clusters, called constellations, that people can use as guides.

Using the star charts
Turn the map so that the month in which you are looking is at the bottom of the chart. If you are in the northern hemisphere face south and, if in the southern hemisphere, face north. Look out for the stars in the centre and lower parts of the chart - you should be able to see them.

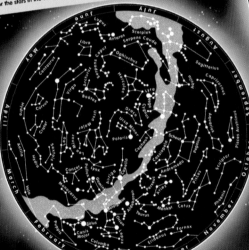

The Northern Hemisphere
The make-up of the night sky looks different depending on which side of the world you are on. The most famous star in the northern hemisphere is the Pole Star (Polaris), which appears to be almost directly above the North Pole. It seems to stay still while other stars move around it. Like many constellations, Ursa Major is named after the Latin name of the creature it resembles in shape - a great bear.

The Southern Hemisphere
Stars on the edge of the northern hemisphere can be seen from the southern hemisphere but not those in the centre. The stars seem more brighter here because there are more star clusters to be seen. The most famous and brightest star is Sirius (the Dog Star), which is part of the Canis Major (Great Dog) constellation.

STAR GUIDE

Your kit contains a special star chart showing the constellations. You can stick the glow-in-the-dark stars in these patterns on your ceiling to create a night sky in your room!

THE NORTHERN HEMISPHERE

The make-up of the night sky looks different depending on which side of the world you are on. The most famous star in the northern hemisphere is the Pole Star (Polaris), which appears to be almost directly above the North Pole. It seems to stay still while other stars move around it. Like many constellations, Ursa Major is named after the Latin name of the creature it resembles in shape – a great bear.

THE SOUTHERN HEMISPHERE

Stars on the edge of the northern hemisphere can be seen from the southern hemisphere but not those in the centre. The stars seem much brighter here because there are more star clusters to be seen. The most famous and brightest star is Sirius (the Dog Star), which is part of the Canis Major (Great Dog) constellation.

STAR GUIDE

The Great Bear

This is seen in the
northern sky all
year round.
The seven stars
to the rear of the bear form
a mini constellation called
the Plough.

The Little Bear

Near the Great Bear is the Little
Bear. At the tip of the Little Bear's
tail is Polaris, the Pole star.

Cassiopeia

The 'W' shape of Cassiopeia, the Queen, is found to the north east of the Pole Star.

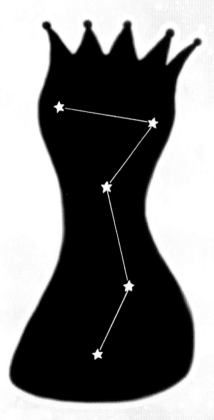

Orion

Orion, the Hunter, fills the sky in January and February. Look for the three stars that form his belt.

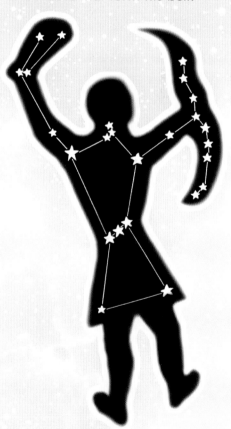

GALAXIES

Galaxies are collections of billions of stars. The Universe is such an enormous place that it contains many millions of galaxies.

Seeing galaxies

In this picture taken by the Hubble Space Telescope, every smudge and dot you can see is a galaxy.

Spiral galaxies

Most of the galaxies we can see have a spiral shape.

Barred spirals

These spiral-type galaxies have a bar-shape in the middle.

Irregular galaxies

These have no regular shape.

Elliptical galaxies

These appear as round or oval shapes.

The Milky Way

You can get a view of our own galaxy – the Milky Way – on a clear night. It looks like a band of milky-white light.

GALAXY PICTURE

Create your own picture of a spiral galaxy. You could hang it on your wall next to your star chart.

You will need:

- a large piece of black card
- white paint
- a paintbrush
- newspaper

Step 1

Ask if there is any old newspaper that no one wants anymore. Lay plenty of it down across your whole work area. Make sure you wear old clothes as this is a messy project!

Place your piece of black card on the newspaper in the middle of your work area.

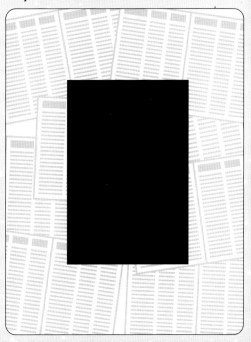

GALAXY PICTURE

Step 2

Dip your paintbrush into the paint and flick it in a splattery pattern all over the black card.

Try to turn your paper as you do this to create a spiral effect.

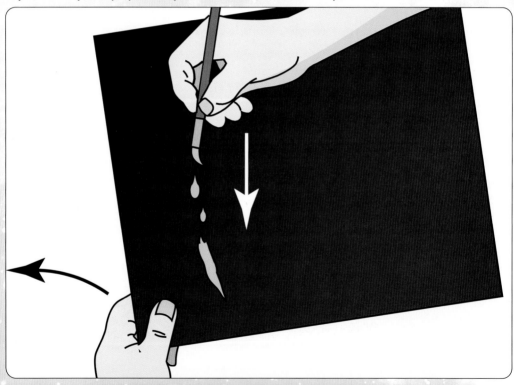

Step 3

Do the same with a few different coloured paints and, once dry, you will have a great picture of a galaxy to hang on your wall. For larger stars just dip the end of your brush in the paint and dot them on.

Tip: You may need to make the paint a bit thinner with some water.

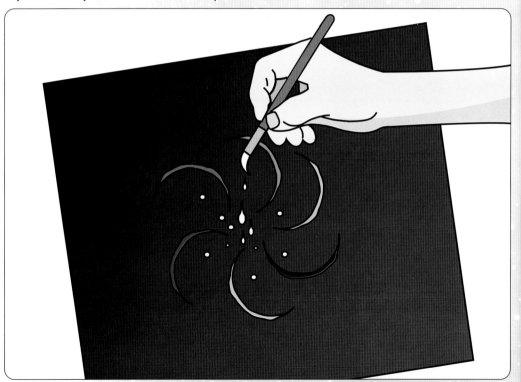

SPACE EXPLORATION

It is very exciting to explore space, and humans have done so for many years. Rockets are used to launch lots of space missions, from buggys to explore the surface of the Moon and Mars to those carrying people to space stations.

One of the most exciting space exploration missions ever, was when three astronauts landed on the Moon watched on television by millions of people.

Space stations are used by astronauts from many countries around the world to conduct lots of different experiments.

DO ALIENS EXIST?

People have always wondered if there is life on other planets. So far, nobody has found any signs that aliens, other species, exist.

Looking for Life

Scientists use radio telescopes to look for signs of alien life. These huge dishes search for signals from outer space.

We are Here!

Space probes sent into space carry information about the Earth and humans. If aliens find the probes, they will know what we look like.

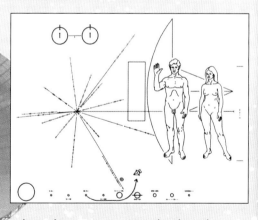

This plaque was attached to the exterior of the Pioneer 10 & 11 spacecrafts.

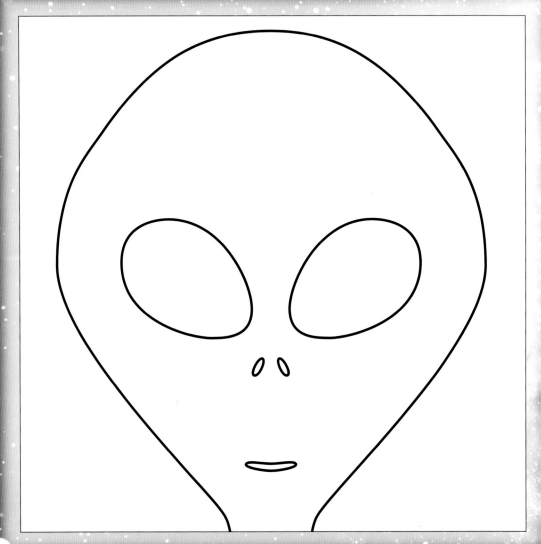

ALIEN MASK

Frighten your friends with this spooky alien mask.

You will need:

- paints • a bowl
- kitchen paper or newpaper
- a piece of cardboard
- PVA glue • scissors

Step 1

Copy the shape of the template mask, shown opposite, onto a piece of cardboard.

Be sure to make it much bigger than this one, though, so that it covers the whole of your face.

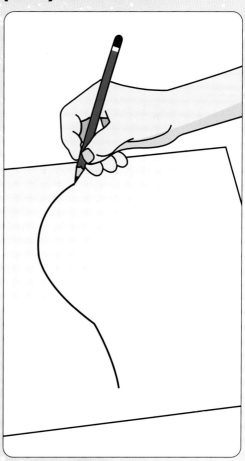

ALIEN MASK

Step 2

Soak the strips of paper in a mixture of PVA glue diluted in water so it looks like milk. Squeeze out any excess liquid. Build up cheekbones, eyes and mouth with layers of scrunched-up paper and then place strips flat on top of these areas to make the surface smooth. Leave to dry.

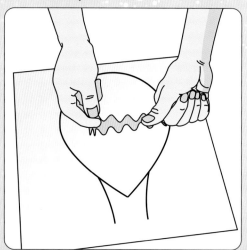

Step 3

Paint the whole of the mask grey and leave the paint to dry. Paint the oval eyes and the mouth with black paint, as shown below.

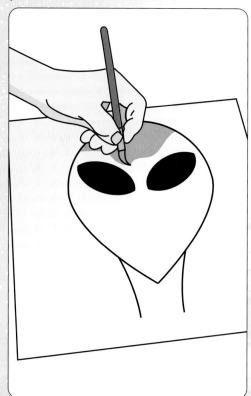

Step 4

When the grey paint has dried, you may wish to apply a layer of white paint. Ask an adult to cut your mask out.

Step 5

Holding the mask in front of your face, creep up behind your friends or your family and quietly, gently tap them on the back.

They will be really spooked when they turn around to see an alien facing them!

FASCINATING FACTS

The Moon is about 240,000 miles (384,400 km) from Earth. It would take almost 3 years to get there on your bicycle!

The planets close to the Sun such as Mercury, are far too hot to live on. Other planets further away from the Sun, such as Pluto, are far too cold to live on.

A day on Jupiter is less than 10 hours long.

A huge meteorite fell to Earth about 25,000 years ago. The crater it made in the Arizona Desert as it landed is around 1,300 m across and 175 m deep!

Earth takes around 365 days to go around the Sun and this makes up one year. A year on Mercury lasts only 88 days but on Pluto it lasts for 250 of our years.